New City Books

The New City Books series explores the intersection of architecture, landscape architecture, infrastructure, and planning in the redevelopment of the civic realm. Focusing on government sponsorship of design, the study of weak-market cities, contemporary American housing, and the role of a research university as a resource and collaborator, the series highlights the formative nature of innovative design and the necessity for strategies that trigger public and private support.

The New City Books series includes:

From the Ground Up
Innovative Green Homes

Formerly Urban
Projecting Rust Belt Futures

New Public Works
Architecture, Planning, and Politics

Modern American Housing
High-Rise, Reuse, Infill

American City "X"
Syracuse after the Master Plan

AMERICAN CITY "X" SYRACUSE AFTER THE MASTER PLAN

Edited by Mark Robbins

With contributions by
Barry Bergdoll
Nancy Cantor
Julia Czerniak
Mark Robbins

Syracuse University
School of Architecture
and
Princeton Architectural Press

Published by
Princeton Architectural Press
37 East Seventh Street
New York, New York 10003
Visit our website at www.papress.com.

Syracuse University School of Architecture
Slocum Hall
Syracuse, New York 13244
www.soa.syr.edu

Printed and bound in China by 1010 Printing
International

17 16 15 14 4 3 2 1 First edition

Series Editor: Mark Robbins

Writer and Researcher: Rachel Somerstein

Design: Pentagram

Project Editor: Dan Simon

Special thanks to: Mariam Aldhahi, Meredith
Baber, Sara Bader, Nicola Bednarek Brower,
Janet Behning, Megan Carey, Carina Cha,
Andrea Chlad, Barbara Darko, Benjamin
English, Russell Fernandez, Will Foster,
Jan Hartman, Jan Haux, Diane Levinson,
Jennifer Lippert, Amrita Marino, Katharine
Myers, Jaime Nelson, Lauren Palmer, Jay
Sacher, Rob Shaeffer, Andrew Stepanian,
Marielle Suba, and Joseph Weston of
Princeton Architectural Press
　　　　　—Kevin C. Lippert, publisher

The New City Books series is made possible
by a grant from the Rockefeller Foundation.
Additional funding is provided by the
Syracuse University School of Architecture,
Judith Greenberg Seinfeld, the National
Endowment for the Arts, The Richard H.
Driehaus Foundation, the Graham Foundation
for Advanced Studies in the Fine Arts, the
New York State Council for the Arts, Deutsche
Bank Americas Foundation, Furthermore: a
program of the J. M. Kaplan Fund, and the
Central New York Community Foundation.

Library of Congress
Cataloging-in-Publication Data

American city X : Syracuse after the master
plan / Mark Robbins. — First edition.

pages cm. — (New city books)
ISBN 978-1-61689-106-0 (hardback)
1. Architecture and society—New York
(State)—Syracuse. 2. City planning—Social
aspects—New York (State)—Syracuse. 3.
Syracuse (N.Y.)—Buildings, structures, etc. I.
Robbins, Mark, 1956- editor of compilation. II.
Robbins, Mark, 1956- Optimistic urbanism.
NA2543.S6A44 2013

711'.40974766—dc23

2012049340

Contents

FOREWORD
NANCY
CANTOR

We are living during a time when so many American cities, especially those of the Rust Belt, are challenged to make the most of what the sociologist Saskia Sassen has called our "cityness"—the "intersection of differences" that is the very foundation of urbanity. For so many years, that intersection was utterly abandoned as cities like Syracuse were partitioned by highways and eviscerated by misguided policies that eroded our social networks, our public school systems, and our industrial base while increasing the volume of tax-delinquent and vacant land and crumbling infrastructure. Such policies left city governments with impossibly small operating budgets, as the tax base fled to suburbs increasingly separated from, rather than joined with, adjacent city centers.

But in the city of Syracuse, we have taken up the challenge to reclaim our "cityness." A key strategy is for our anchor institutions—our colleges and universities and other place-based, long-standing cultural, civic, and economic foundations of the community—to step up and embrace that role. You might say that for Syracuse University living up to our anchor role entails reclaiming our "universityness." We're bringing our intellectual capital to the table as we join with partners from other sectors to help reclaim Syracuse's intersections of difference, making what the Brookings Institution's Bruce Katz calls "transformative investments."

When we do this, we're strategic. We look for opportunities to play to our disciplinary strengths, as well as those of our partners. As an anchor institution, we strive to do things that are socially and physically sustainable, particularly commissioning and fostering urban design that is both inspired and sustainable. You can find examples all across the city: from the east side, where our Syracuse Center of Excellence (CoE) headquarters, a LEED-Platinum design by Toshiko Mori, stands on the site of a reclaimed brownfield; to downtown, where our

alumnus Richard Gluckman turned one of Syracuse's ugliest
buildings, a formerly windowless furniture warehouse, into one
of our most beautiful, a landmark of light and color; to the Near
Westside, where the School of Architecture and the CoE collabo-
rated on an international design competition for sustainable
and affordable single-family homes, three of which have been
built and are now occupied. Tying these new landmarks together
is our emerging, signature strip of cultural development—the
Connective Corridor—where we're collaborating with the city
of Syracuse to weave technology and sustainability through the
city's remarkably resilient fabric of cultural institutions and parks
from University Hill all the way across town.

So, the challenges that our cities face may be great, but I would
suggest that a city like Syracuse is the ideal place to try to find
solutions: small enough to be able to see the effects of transformative investments in a reasonable amount of time, and large enough
for strategies to be tested meaningfully so we know they can be
scaled up. As we reclaim our cityness, we are also reclaiming the
future for all of us. Exploring solutions is what this book is all
about. It is one contribution to an ongoing dialogue, and we very
much look forward to learning from and with its readers.

PREFACE

The idea for this book grew out of an exhibition that took place at the Syracuse University School of Architecture in late 2007. Curated by Mark Robbins, the school's former dean, and organized by UPSTATE: A Center for Design, Research, and Real Estate, the exhibition included built and planned projects on the campus of the university and in the city of Syracuse, notable both for the caliber of designers involved and the speed with which they emerged. The intention of the exhibition was to demonstrate that innovative and compelling works of architecture change the way a city functions and enhance the way it is perceived.

This work has been made possible by the support and vision for "scholarship in action" as defined by Syracuse University's chancellor, Nancy Cantor. The university and the School of Architecture have been positioned as significant forces in Syracuse, creating a model for the ways in which the profession and the academy can spur revitalization in the midsize, post-industrial city. The projects presented here were developed with a range of clients and a variety of strategies, driven by academic, civic, and nonprofit groups as well as private real estate concerns, often working in partnership. The projects—from landscape architecture to building and infrastructure, institutional to residential, renovation to new construction—address issues of sustainability, material and formal experimentation, and programmatic invention.

Threading the complex relationship between engagement and curricular work, the university and the School of Architecture have developed an asset-based model for interaction, understanding local resources to include campus, city, and region. The creation of UPSTATE: by Robbins within the School of Architecture, as well as initiatives such as the Connective Corridor and the Near Westside Initiative, has attracted public and private funding as well as broader public awareness of the significance of design in urban revitalization strategies.

Projects incorporate multiple approaches to commissioning public and private work that involves nationally recognized design firms, often with the participation of students, visiting critics, and faculty in designing and building. Community engagement has been critical, as has the political and financial support of local, regional, and federal governments. These projects have also helped develop capacity and elevate the profile of the local contracting, engineering, and professional design communities through new design partnerships.

Architectural aspirations for Syracuse are not new. As Barry Bergdoll writes in his essay, Syracuse once served as the model city for postwar America. In May 1943, the editors of *Fortune* and *Architectural Forum* selected Syracuse as the typical American city and solicited ideas from top architects for the complete redevelopment of the city after the war that were presented in "New Buildings for 194X." This vision of the future for Syracuse included buildings by such leading midcentury architects as Charles Eames, Louis Kahn, and Ludwig Mies van der Rohe.

Much has changed since 1943, including the idea of the master plan as a wholesale replacement of the urban fabric. A strategic form of intervention, what Robbins refers to as "optimistic urbanism" in his essay in this volume, offers intriguing opportunities. Recognizing the impossibility of rebuilding a nineteenth-century city, Julia Czerniak, the inaugural director of UPSTATE:, explores other responsive models for contemporary urbanity in her essay, "Liquid Assets," where she describes how landscape urbanism projects using water, an abundant resource in the region, have the potential to organize and transform the city. Syracuse offers a model for the ways in which the intersection of social, economic, and educational innovation can be made manifest in the built environment.

The development of cities takes many hands, and the projects in Syracuse are evidence of the creative drive and commitment of many individuals. Valued partners and colleagues have included Marilyn Higgins, Syracuse University's vice president for community engagement and economic development; Kerry Quaglia, executive director of Home HeadQuarters; Ed Bogusz, executive director of the Center of Excellence; Eric Beattie, director of campus planning, design, and construction;

Julia Czerniak; and Paul Driscoll, commissioner of Syracuse's
Department of Neighborhood and Business Development.
This work has been possible only because of the supportive
framework at the university created by the dynamic vision of
Chancellor Nancy Cantor.

ACKNOWLEDG-
MENTS

The New City Books series, of which this publication is a part, is made possible by a grant from the Rockefeller Foundation. Additional funding is provided by the Syracuse University School of Architecture, the National Endowment for the Arts, the Richard H. Driehaus Foundation, the Graham Foundation for Advanced Studies in the Fine Arts, the New York State Council for the Arts, Deutsche Bank Americas Foundation, Furthermore: a program of the J. M. Kaplan Fund, and the Central New York Community Foundation. We are grateful to all of these funders for their support.

This book would not have been possible without a committed group at the School of Architecture. Many thanks to Nilus Klingel, Syracuse University Engagement Fellow, for his hard work and positive attitude. For their encouragement and support of the New City Books series, we would like to thank Julia Czerniak, Assistant Dean Katryn Hansen, and especially Mary Kate O'Brien, director of communications and media relations, for taking on the project with skill and good humor.

At Princeton Architectural Press, we would like to thank Jennifer and Kevin Lippert for their interest in the New City Books series and its ambitions, and Dan Simon for seeing this book and the series through to fruition. The design of the books was especially important given the topic, and the way they look and read is the outcome of many productive conversations with Michael Bierut and Pentagram. We are grateful for Michael's calm intellect and wit throughout the process, as well as for the graphic talents of designer Hamish Smyth. Finally, we have benefited from Karen Stein's acumen and counsel in the development of the series as a whole, and from Kate Norment's management of the series with a steady yet firm hand. This entire team has become a small community, without which this book and this series could not have come into being.

Mark Robbins
Former dean, Syracuse University School of Architecture

ARCHITECTURE OF 194X
BARRY BERGDOLL

Within months of the U.S. entry into World War II, Syracuse had been targeted. Not by enemy forces, but by the editors of *Fortune* and *Architectural Forum* magazines, who made Syracuse the subject of a model approach to comprehensive planning. Their Fortune-Forum Experimental Department sought to bring together leading economists, planners, and architects to plan an anticipatory attack on what they foresaw as the challenges of the home front's postwar economy. This "Architecture of 194X," as they labeled a war effort that they were sure would last less than a decade, advanced Syracuse as the model city, because as "a busy industrial community of 200,000, it has many of the characteristics and problems of a thriving city of medium size. It has a highly diversified industry, an excellent university, no real slums."[1]

If enacted, the editors' plans would have innovated not only individual building types but also American downtowns in a renaissance for urban fabric that had suffered years of economic depression, only to languish further as resources were reallocated to the war effort. Some seventy years later, it is worth looking back to the Architecture of 194X not to imagine what might have been but as a point of reference for today's architects, educators, economists, and planners, who in recent years have come together to conceive the future of the Rust Belt—of which Syracuse is, once again, a prime example.

To develop the Architecture of 194X, the city government of Syracuse, including, notably, Sergei Grimm, head of the Syracuse City Planning Commission, worked hand in hand with editors from the two magazines. While *Fortune* undertook the economic modeling—summarized in a May 1943 article titled "Syracuse Tackles Its Future"[2]—the noted architect and designer George Nelson, an editor at *Architectural Forum*, directed the physical remodeling. The results, published in the May 1943 issue of *Architectural Forum*, a special issue titled "New Buildings for 194X," show a hypothetical Syracuse to be replanned with widened streets, pedestrian plazas and thoroughfares, and silos of parking

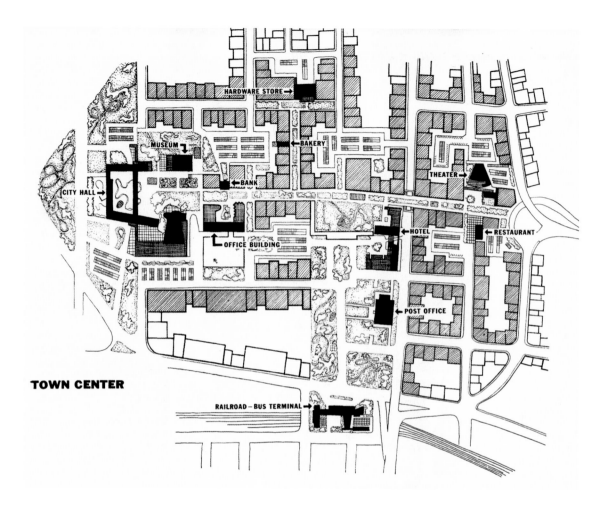

Above: Diagram of proposed town
center for "New Buildings for 194X."
From "New Buildings for 194X,"
Architectural Forum (May 1943), p. 71

Opposite, top and bottom: Rendering
of museum facade by Mies van der
Rohe; suggested placement of artwork
in proposed museum. From "New
Buildings for 194X," *Architectural Forum*
(May 1943), pp. 84–85

Aerial view of Syracuse with plaza site
plan, ca. 1950. From *The Community
Plaza, City of Syracuse/County of
Onondaga*, n.d. [c. 1958–59], p. 15

lots at the perimeter of the district to remove car traffic from an area to be fitted out with new institutions to integrate cultural and commercial life. Under the direction of the planners Russell Van Nest Black and Hugh Pomeroy, Nelson worked with the architects Henry Churchill and Richard Neutra, among others, all of whom met with local planning groups in Syracuse to fulfill the mantra announced in *Fortune*: "Our economy must find a peace production program that approaches the war program."[3]

A total of twenty-three buildings were commissioned for this ideal Syracuse, including a hotel by Oscar Stonorov and Louis Kahn, a city hall by Charles Eames, an office building by Pietro Belluschi, an airport by Antonin Raymond, a gasoline station by William Lescaze, and a hospital by Hugh Stubbins. Syracuse might have become the Columbus, Indiana, of the late 1940s, showcasing the work of many of the leading architectural talents of America. Perhaps the most enduring fame would accrue to Mies's design for a museum for Syracuse, which has often been discussed as a forerunner of his New National Gallery in Berlin but is almost never associated with the replanning of Syracuse.[4] Most intriguing were the commissioning of a "house factory" from Caleb Hornbostel to provide prefabricated houses for the city and its surrounding suburbs and the design of a shopping center by the Los Angeles–based team of Victor Gruenbaum and Elise Krummeck, the only woman designer on the project.

Soon thereafter Gruenbaum would change his name to Gruen and emerge as one of the great shopping-center designers and planners of America's postwar boom, the veritable father of the shopping malls that were to kill the very downtowns *Fortune* and *Architectural Forum* set out to revive. More significant, he would in the 1950s take over the adaptation of the recommendations first studied in the national press, then in the Syracuse-Onondaga Post-War Planning Council's report for the city, published in 1944, to create the Community Plaza that was the core of Syracuse's postwar urban renewal scheme.[5] The Community Plaza—a mixed-use government and cultural center—was to be the anchor of an enormous 101-acre urban renewal project on the Near Eastside immediately adjacent to downtown.[6] As demolition was scheduled for the inner-city neighborhood, plans were afoot to attract suburbanites back downtown to a new cultural plaza, with easy freeway access and parking. In addition to a new city hall and county offices, cultural facilities, including a concert hall and museums of industry, natural history, and the fine arts, were to surround a series of linked pedestrian plazas stretching over a superblock created by suppressing through streets and flanking the area north and south with multi-story parking garages.

Gruen proposed a careful staging of construction for minimum disruption of downtown traffic and maximum early appeal to the regional audience. The final stage, which ultimately never arrived, called for middle-class high-rise housing immediately to the east of the cultural center. While Gruen sketched all the buildings in the master plan, it was clear that, following the example of *Architectural Forum*, individual buildings would be given to leading architects.

The key result was a new museum—not, however, the museum Mies designed in 1943 when he turned down the invitation from *Architectural Forum*'s editors to design a church and proposed instead a new kind of museum, in which "the entire building's space would be available for larger groups, encouraging a more representative use of the museum than is customary today, and creating a noble background for the civic and cultural life of the whole community." Rather, this new conceptualization of the postwar museum would be written into the program many years later for the Everson Museum of Art, designed by the then up-and-coming architect I. M. Pei, a virtually unsung masterpiece in a very different vein of the renaissance of museum architecture in postwar America.[7]

With its shrinking population and oversize infrastructure, Syracuse bears little resemblance to the hypothetical ideal sketched out here. Yet the city's troubled urban fabric—which so resembles the same ills faced by cities throughout the Rust Belt—lends itself to the kind of meaningful intervention imagined by the architects of 194X. Once again, Syracuse has the opportunity to function as a model city for all those American towns struggling to reinvent themselves in the postindustrial age.

1   "New Buildings for 194X," *Architectural Forum* (May 1943): 69–189.

2   "Syracuse Tackles Its Future," *Fortune* 27 (May 1943): 120–23. For a comprehensive
     study of the planning implications of 194X, see Andrew M. Shanken, *194X: Architecture,
     Planning, and Consumer Culture on the American Home Front* (Minneapolis: University
     of Minnesota Press, 2009).

3   "Syracuse Tackles Its Future," 121.

4   On Mies's "Museum for a Small City," see Phyllis Lambert, ed., *Mies in America* (New
     York: Abrams, 2001), 426–28; see also Neil Levine, "The Significance of Facts: Mies's
     Collages Up Close and Personal," *Assemblage* 37 (December 1998): 70–101.

5   See Syracuse-Onondaga Post-War Planning Council, *Community Facilities: Preliminary*
     (Syracuse: Syracuse-Onondaga Post-War Planning Council, 1944); Blair Associates,
     Onondaga-Syracuse Metropolitan Area Planning Studies, 10 vols. (Syracuse, 1961–62);
     The Community Plaza, City of Syracuse/County of Onondaga, undated (c. 1958–59)
     report signed by coordinating architects Ketcham-Miller-Arnold/Gordon P. Schopfer
     and planning and design consultants Victor Gruen Associates/Raymond and May
     Associates. Copies of all three documents are in the Avery Architectural and Fine Arts
     Library, Columbia University, New York.

6   *The Community Plaza, City of Syracuse/County of Onondaga*. The Syracuse project
     is mentioned but not treated in any significant detail in M. Jeffrey Hardwick, *Mall
     Maker: Victor Gruen, Architect of an American Dream* (Philadelphia: University of
     Pennsylvania Press, 2004).

7   Barry Bergdoll, "I. M. Pei, Marcel Breuer, Edward Larrabee Barnes, and the New
     American Museum Design of the 1960s," in *A Modernist Museum in Perspective:
     The East Building, National Gallery of Art* (Washington, D.C.: National Gallery of
     Art, 2009), 107–23.

OPTIMISTIC URBANISM: MAKING OTHER PLANS

MARK ROBBINS

The city represented in the modernist urban plan known as "New Buildings for 194X" reflects an optimism about the potential of remaking the American city following the Depression and the expected end of World War II. Embedded in it are a set of formal and social propositions and assumptions about the way a new city would look and work. The aspirations of this iteration came in the form of the superblock tailored to the car, with large-scale infrastructure that would enable the commute between atomized zones of work and home. After the publication of this plan, more than twenty years would elapse before its spirit would be given concrete form, if only in part. As a midsize "thriving" city, Syracuse was selected as the base for 194X; in recent years it has also proved to be in some ways a prototype for cities across the United States and Europe whose economic roots have moved elsewhere and whose areas now exceed their populations.

Just out of the frame of the site plan as it would be realized in Syracuse lay fragments of earlier approaches to urban design and reform, which preceded it by fifty years. Like a sampler of American planning, each set of forms expressed a vision for efficiency, order, and commodity. And like other earlier city maps, the one from 1938, for example, is composed of a clear set of grids punctuated by the figural spaces of the City Beautiful movement, with fragments of diagonal avenues and surviving traces of the Erie Canal that parallel later rail lines. By the late 1960s the density had changed, reflecting shifts in the thinning population. The original grids are legible, though cleaved now by the interstate and a ring road encircling the region, and complemented by an abundance of parking lots, while one-way streets created by traffic engineers serve as high-speed thoroughfares in and out of town.

On a site occupying Syracuse's Fifteenth Ward, previously home to a mostly African American population, construction began in 1965 on the Everson Museum of Art as the centerpiece of the ambitious Community Plaza urban renewal project. Marcel Breuer's

Sketch of view looking south from
proposed community plaza. From
*The Community Plaza, City of
Syracuse/County of Onondaga,*
n.d. [c. 1958–59], p. 22

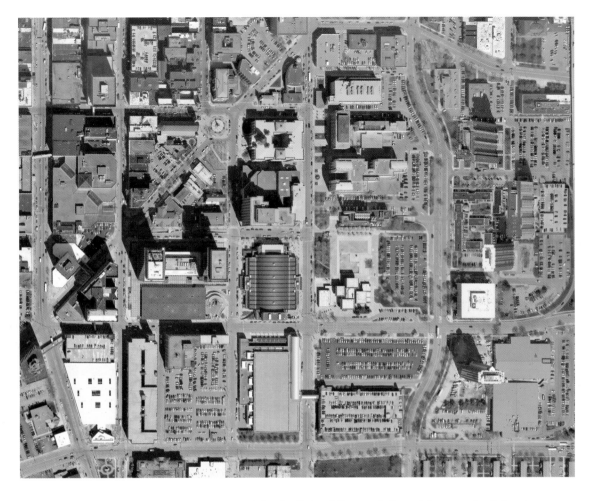

Aerial view of present-day Syracuse

proposal for the Bristol Center followed in 1970. Anticipating President Lyndon B. Johnson's 1966 Model Cities program, the Everson Museum complex reflects a vision of the city as, like the 194X map, a dispersed, modern place, accommodating vast numbers of cars, with gardens and residential and office towers in the place of dense, low-scale neighborhoods. At the heart of what was to be this new district is the cultural institution that was planned as a central locus for the new city. Its expansive plazas speak of the expectation of large crowds, though the district no longer had the local density to support it.

Much of what we see in the form of Syracuse is the result of national housing and transportation policies devised fifty and sixty years ago during a period that saw the release of two critical

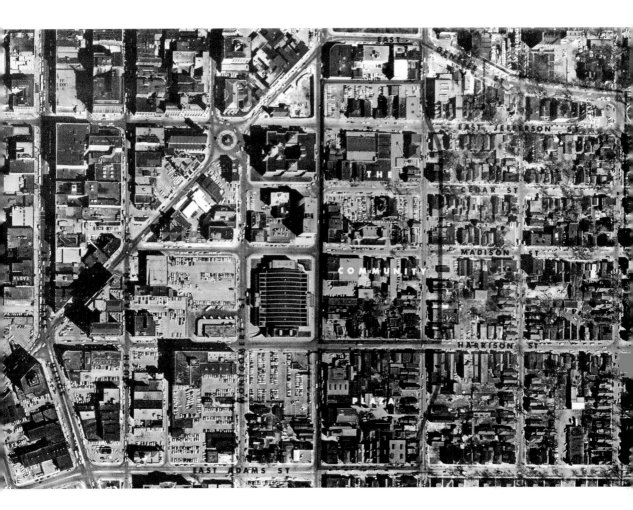

Aerial view of 1950s Syracuse with proposed community plaza.
From *The Community Plaza, City of Syracuse/County of Onondaga*, n.d. [c. 1958–59], p. 11

documents, both by Daniel Patrick Moynihan, assistant secretary of labor: "Guiding Principles for Federal Architecture," released in 1962 under the Kennedy administration, which advocated for the best contemporary design rather than advancing an official style; and, perhaps more famous, "The Negro Family: The Case for National Action," published in 1965 under President Johnson and also known as the Moynihan Report, which related poverty within black communities to a weakening of the family structure. This was a period also influenced by the optimism of the Kennedy era and Johnson's Great Society, whose vision of social life included planning and architecture. That both could factor at the level of policy would have an impact on the shape of American cities and our view of them. The confluence of highway construction (which came relatively late to Syracuse) and urban renewal, with its "slum clearance,"

Syracuse Builds exhibition, 2007,
The Warehouse, Syracuse

the flight of the most economically mobile and mostly white residents, and the loss of industrial and commercial bases, in the city and
the region, combined to create a familiar condition in urban America.
The lessons learned from these initiatives are timely again in light
of the current reconsideration of urban redevelopment policy at
the federal level, which increasingly stresses collaboration between
agencies at the state and local levels through such programs as the
Sustainable Communities Regional Planning Grant, cosponsored
by the Environmental Protection Agency and the Departments of
Transportation and Housing and Urban Development.

Some American cities are already deeply in the process of revising
the impact of earlier planning decisions. Relatively cheap vacant
lots and buildings have been identified as valuable assets for commercial and residential use. Housing development has been recognized as an important method to seed downtowns with permanent
activities rather than transient ones, such as festival events.
The land occupied by superblock malls adjacent to downtowns
has been reallocated, sky bridges over streets have been removed,
pedestrian malls have been made vehicular again, one-way

streets—which make freeways out of surface streets—have been
made two-way.

Cities and regions that have invested intelligently in infrastructure
and guided development projects have longer-term good to show
for this. At the bluntest level it's about what it is and where it's put.
We can learn from the mistakes of earlier planning and are in an
ideal position to select, edit, and curate from a catalog of successful
strategies and inventions of others to make more-informed decisions about our future.

The work in this publication suggests an approach to recrafting
the typical American city now, in its actual postwar, post-urban-
renewal state. Recognizing the lack of massive funds aimed at
renewal as well as the limits of earlier approaches, the method
suggested draws on a variety of physical and social patterns as a
base for strategic interventions that offer the potential for inflec-
tion and linkages at several scales. As opposed to the clean slate
associated with the master plan, more particularized design interventions draw from the social, political, and economic opportunities at hand. It is an urbanism that is, in the best sense, opportunistic. Discrete projects can have a catalytic impact on the existing
urban fabric, with street patterns reconsidered and landscape
used more intensively as part of the planning.

Syracuse ranks 170th nationally and 5th in New York State in
terms of size, with a population that has fallen from a high of
220,000 in 1950 to 145,000 in 2010. The median household income,
$25,000, is less than half the state's median income of $54,500. Not
surprisingly, Syracuse's biggest economic forces are universities
and hospitals—a phenomenon shared by other postindustrial
cities—with Syracuse University and the SUNY Upstate Medical
University at Syracuse as the city's largest employers.

The university is located a bit more than a mile from the city's core,
but the highway and the surrounding terrain heighten the sense of
separation. The gradual reconfiguration of streets and circulation paths within the campus also reflects the influence of the
modern superblock, with closed streets and limited-access roads
insulating the campus from the surrounding streets. The density of
the area around campus has been reduced in favor of suburban satel-
lites within driving distance from the main academic quad. The frag-

mented edges between city and campus intersecting with highway infrastructure create zones of unclaimed and untended space.

All the projects in this volume have been conceived within the past ten years, and many have been completed within that time, employing a variety of means. All required a strategic use of funds, as well as a careful selection of both site and architect. Some of these projects were done through traditional means of site acquisition, commissioning, and/or renovation. Others were built through hybrid funding, with sources including New York State, Syracuse University, and private developers. They are located on campus, in the downtown district, and in locations that span and connect those areas, and they range from buildings to landscapes to infrastructural work. Local architectural and engineering firms have partnered with nationally recognized design firms, building the local capacity and also giving recent graduates greater reasons to stay and work in Syracuse. Collaborative efforts through university-led and private initiatives, with funding from the state and county, endeavor to connect the campus with downtown and to create a path between cultural, civic, and academic sites with landscape and infrastructure projects. At the same time, the university plays host to professionals who teach with expertise in landscape, planning, hydrology, graphic design, and architecture.

Two developments just outside the downtown core make a case for the effectiveness of design and planning expertise paired with economic and political means. The first is the Near Westside, an urban neighborhood in Syracuse comprising some 200 structures, including wood-frame houses, schools, public housing, and large commercial and warehouse buildings. It provides a microcosm of the building types and social fabric of Syracuse, and of neighborhoods found across the country. Though its median household income of $11,500 makes it one of the poorest census tracts in the United States, as a whole it offers a scale like the city itself, in which modest projects will have an impact. The Near Westside Initiative (NWSI) was founded as a nonprofit development corporation by Syracuse University to work intensively in this community. The university was instrumental in providing $13.8 million through the state as a nucleus for building acquisition and construction, with funds divided among the Syracuse University School of Architecture, the NWSI, and the Center of Excellence (CoE), a state-funded facility devoted to technology.

The Near Westside was also the site of From the Ground Up,
a competition for new sustainable houses organized in 2008 by the
School of Architecture partnering with the NWSI, the CoE, and
Home HeadQuarters, a private nonprofit housing agency. The purpose of the competition was to create models for high-energy-per-
formance homes and to encourage a reconsideration of the city's
approach to density. Zoning and density are critical to the discussion, as the existing social-service models and city zoning policies
have encouraged demolition, larger lot sizes, and the fusing of
multiple lots into single-home sites with asphalt parking pads rather
than on-street parking. Landlords and home owners are encouraged to acquire adjacent lots for use as side yards, further reducing the number of dwellings per block. The character and density of
the walkable neighborhood of 33-by-100-foot lots have been eroded
in favor of a suburban model, which is considered more marketable.

Of the seven finalists, three new houses—by Architecture Research
Office/Della Valle Bernheimer, Cook + Fox Architects, and Onion
Flats—have been built and sold. They sit amid preexisting houses
on lots of original size and feature a varied massing typical of the
neighborhood. As part of a parallel project, students are working with
the architect Frederick Stelle and the professor Timothy Stenson
and in partnership with Home HeadQuarters on the renovation of
vacant homes on the same block. VIP Structures, which has expressed
early support, will build these houses. This is a small-scale intervention, and efforts to replicate this work through more sustainable financing are under discussion. The hope is to create a model
within this ensemble of old and new homes on dense, replanted
lots to demonstrate the coexistence of innovative new structures on
empty lots and the preservation of the historic fabric. This diversity
has attracted new residents and retained preexisting ones as new
home buyers. The former industrial buildings that line one edge
of the neighborhood will become a cultural anchor for the area.
A 220,000-square-foot heavy timber warehouse, renovated by
Koning Eizenberg Architecture with King + King Architects, will
become the offices and studio for the region's public broadcasting
station, WCNY, as well as the home of a national adult literacy organization; lofts are planned for the second phase of the project. Another,
smaller warehouse, the 30,000-square-foot Lincoln Supply
Building, has been renovated by Brininstool + Lynch as a mixed-use
building composed of leased offices and live/work lofts.

Red House Arts Center and Subcat
Studios, downtown Syracuse

Across the street, an earlier renovation, known as the Warehouse, evolved out of the need for swing space for the School of Architecture, but it also marked a significant engagement of the university with downtown. The university's chancellor supported the purchase of the building and its redevelopment, and in 2006 Gluckman Mayner Architects renovated the space, creating a new home for the School of Architecture and programs of the university's College of Visual and Performing Arts, as well as library storage, a community art space, and a gallery. The building abuts one of the few pedestrian-oriented areas in the city, and a twenty-four-hour shuttle links the facility with the campus, downtown, and various cultural institutions—a proximity that will be reinforced with the phased construction of the Connective Corridor.

Even more recently, the Warehouse has been renovated once again, this time into an art and design center as well as additional studio space for the School of Architecture and the offices of its program UPSTATE: A Center for Design, Research, and Real Estate. Private developers, such as the Pioneer Companies, have acquired adjacent parcels and built new buildings, including

Washington Station, which houses a 300-person engineering firm that moved from a suburban setting to downtown. King + King, one of the nation's oldest architecture firms, moved its sixty-person office to a vacant building that it renovated to state-of-the-art green standards. Across the street, an alternative arts center, the Red House, expanded its footprint with the renovation of a warehouse by Fiedler Marciano Architecture, which houses recording studios and artist residences. At the risk of oversimplification, these projects can be read as textbook redevelopment strategy, relying on a catalyst—in this case, the university's very public investment in and commitment to downtown through the Warehouse renovation—to help attract further development. The university has been a conduit for much of the initial funding for projects like the Warehouse and WCNY, which has come from a mix of public and private sources. The university has also been critical in encouraging the interchange of ideas and practices, creating a new position of vice president of community engagement and economic development to oversee and develop both the Connective Corridor and the Near Westside Initiative. This has brought together different kinds of projects, disparate groups, and a range of expertise, from

Cluster of newly developed projects on the western edge of downtown Syracuse

law to workforce and retail development, combining impassioned, community-based work with rigorous architecture, landscape architecture, urban design, and art, all used in projective ways.

This approach to urbanism is more complex and granular than earlier steps toward urban renewal, not unlike the university's current interaction with the city versus a more traditional institutional presence. The resulting spaces allow differences to read simultaneously so that the familiar and the unexpected coexist—from the physical form of the city to its uses of technology and social organization. In other words, the layers of the city are legible. Such opportunistic urbanism does not appear as one homogeneous and smooth construction, but instead allows for evidence of the past alongside an apparently radical future. The friction generated between disparate things is positive, an essential element of urban life.

There are literally hundreds of cities across the country that are in the midst of remaking themselves. Those that have done best, like Portland and Pittsburgh, have capitalized on honest assets rather than themes. Cities are works in progress. Invention can change the perception of a place and the way it is programmed. Cities that have taken leaps rather than small steps have done better in attracting more development and slowing population decline, especially among younger residents. The approach in Syracuse is incremental in part by necessity, because of the financial as well as jurisdictional challenges posed by a single massive redevelopment project. Syracuse University, as an economic force and as a draw for population, provides one of the anchors. In an era in which many local governments have been divested of professional expertise, the university has an increasing role to play and can be the interlocutor between private market interests and civic goals. It can influence longer-range thinking, beyond political agendas and immediate economic gain.

Several hundred million dollars have been leveraged through the projects spearheaded by Syracuse University, which are decidedly smaller in scale than mall development or major infrastructure projects. Each project has resulted in progressive and innovative architecture while productively engaging the local community. In urban design terms these projects have developed quickly, and collectively they make a case for ways in which scarce funds can be leveraged to create positive change on multiple fronts: academic, economic, and community based. These various projects show the potential and power of incremental change and the benefits of partnership across a broad range of institutions and constituencies. In this way the public realm is indeed shaped by the many citizens of the city. Developers certainly have an important role to play, but their voices (and resources) should not be isolated from those of other critical decision makers. Architects, scholars, and educators have the ability to show alternatives that are instructive in the civic realm.

In Syracuse there has been a particular set of alignments: the market; social and political will; a progressive, committed chancellor who encourages broad interdisciplinary work and understands architecture's potential role; a school of architecture oriented toward challenging standard assumptions about community-based work; and, importantly, a community with leaders ready to work to make new things happen. These are the specifics of this place. Other places across the world have constellations of options, and it takes an opportunistic eye to read the potential within existing assets.

The argument about the worth of downtown was won years ago in many American cities, and energies have been increasingly directed at the remediation of the early suburbs themselves, this first ring having inherited conditions associated with the center city. In smaller, postindustrial cities like Syracuse, with smaller populations and poorer tax bases, alternative approaches and political faith are still needed to reconfigure development practices in the downtown core. The advantages, however, are that the scale here is more manageable, and over the past thirty years there has been an ample array of projects nationwide to draw from.

Perhaps the X factor in that early map is a placeholder, a pro tempore signifier for the thing we don't quite know. It is the independent variable that can define a place and suggest opportunities to intercede in multiple ways. Where the challenges are greatest, in areas that do not reflect investment at the public level, the most innovative thinking and building are needed in concert with market investment directed in productive ways. Building not only is the outward sign of change but also participates in making change happen.

LIQUID ASSETS: LANDSCAPE, WATER, AND URBAN CHANGE

JULIA CZERNIAK

In the deindustrialized city, landscape is playing an ever-increasing role as the organizer of large-scale projects that effect positive change. Landscape urbanism has emerged as a way to, through design, align the natural environment—topography, hydrology, vegetation, wind patterns, and so on—with structures and systems of the city. Although the term "landscape urbanism" is relatively new, we are reminded that the practice is not. For example, Frederick Law Olmsted thought of urban parks as systems of infrastructure that moved people, water, and waste. The discipline of landscape urbanism suggests a particular culture of the land that engages infrastructure with complex processes of our environment.

In Syracuse, New York, two projects—the Near Westside Neighborhood Plan and the revitalization of Onondaga Creek—rely on landscape elements, structures, and processes as the framework of their organization. In addition, they hinge on leveraging an asset that Syracuse has in abundance: water. Syracuse, which ranks 170th on the list of U.S. cities by size, receives more snow on average—nearly ten feet—than any other large city. In addition, the sun shines a mere sixty-three days a year, and the average annual precipitation is forty inches. Rainfall, like snow, is distributed evenly, almost in daily doses as the season dictates. Along with these conditions are associated weather effects such as perpetually gray skies, long winters, and a bleak-looking urban landscape.

This seemingly dismal picture comes, however, with a bright side when design innovation turns liabilities into assets. The Near Westside Neighborhood Plan uses stormwater infrastructure as a way to provide civic improvements to an underserved urban community. Efforts to revitalize Onondaga Creek reframe an undervalued waterway as the new spine of the city. Both projects employ progressive local design practices as well as state and local funding. The first project was done through the Syracuse University School of Architecture's UPSTATE: A Center for Design, Research, and Real Estate, which focuses on strategies to improve the urban life of formerly urban cities; the second project was completed by a team organized by the Syracuse design firm CLEAR.[1]

UPSTATE:'s work explores infrastructure as an asset-based and economical way to restore urbanity in the Near Westside neighborhood of Syracuse. Like many other shrinking cities, Syracuse has devolved so radically because of economic, demographic, and physical change that it can now be considered "formerly urban."[2] The city's population has been shrinking for decades, as evidenced by loss of city fabric, diminishment of social welfare networks, erosion of public schools, loss of industry, increasing amounts of tax delinquency and vacant land, and crumbling infrastructure. Although the environment of partially occupied urban fabric and parking surfaces produced through these processes is disparate, it is joined by an active downtown and an emerging visual and performing arts infrastructure. Nonetheless, the resulting landscape is not particularly promising for vibrant urban life.

Syracuse is an apt context for UPSTATE:'s exploration not simply because of its challenging social and spatial context but also because of the monies in place in the city for infrastructural improvements. For example, the Near Westside neighborhood is located in a sewer shed that makes it eligible for funds associated with the Onondaga County Green Improvement Fund (GIF). This financial assistance program enables green infrastructure projects to be installed on eligible privately owned properties in certain sewer sheds. GIF supports the development of stormwater mitigation techniques such as biofilter curb extensions, stormwater swales, and rain gardens.[3] All of these measures can significantly improve the ecological health of cities by reducing the volume of water in combined sewer systems that, when overtaxed, force untreated sewage into streams. What is missing, however, from these often cited and regularly funded strategies is consideration of their civic benefits—where design can contribute to activating urban life.

The first focus of the neighborhood plan is Wyoming Street. It is a typical local street in the Near Westside, but it will play a greater role in the future of the community by becoming the major cultural street, edged by publicly programmed renovated warehouses on its east side and housing on its west. Our design approach aims to hybridize ecological performance with the urban ambitions of an avenue. "Avenue" here is used in its traditional sense, as a straight road edged by a line of trees. Drawing on its French root *venir* ("to come"), which emphasizes arriving at a landscape or architectural feature, we anchor the street on its north and south ends with elements that both manage and highlight stormwater.

On the north end of the street are cast-in-place concrete containments that double as tree pits and infiltration sites. Surface runnels scored into the pavement system lead to a water feature constituted by gathered and recycled rain. A simple extension of the basin's concrete pour serves as the foundation for seating made of molded plywood. This is configured to facilitate relaxing, viewing, and napping and thus to integrate activity with the engineered system. A civic use is combined with an ecological purpose in a small package that can be repeated along the street in response to desire and resources (fig., p. 44).[4]

The south end of the street is marked by a new urban space that reconfigures pedestrians and cars in the parking lot of a local supermarket and produces an updated image for an underwhelming amenity. Stormwater from the supermarket's roof and from the parking lot is gathered in biofilter pockets—planted with local grasses and perennials—along the street edge. Modular paving enhances the entrance to the market while calming traffic. Most significant in the design is the organizational banding of permeable and impermeable paving that highlights rain when it falls and directs it toward custom-built protective "nests" that elevate the parking planting to a design installation. This language is repeated, at a different scale, as the site's bollards. Together these strategies both manage stormwater on-site and provide a well-designed civic amenity for the community that would not have been possible without the local funding source (figs., p. 45).

The second project, the revitalization of Onondaga Creek, is a complex and ongoing effort with many partners. An original vision, the Onondaga Creek Conceptual Revitalization Plan, was spearheaded by the Onondaga Environmental Institute and called for large-scale planning efforts to improve the creek. The effort described here led to city officials securing funding from the U.S. Department of State for the preparation and implementation of a Local Waterfront Revitalization Program, which refers to both the planning document created by a community and the program established to

Above: Rendering of concrete
infiltration system to recycle rainwater
and create seating on north end
of Wyoming Street

Opposite, top: Details of stormwater
collection system

Opposite, bottom: Rendering of new
urban space and plantings

implement the plan.[5] In producing a community consensus and
a unified vision, its benefits are twofold. The first is the planning
document itself, along with initial implementation projects that
serve to make urban waterways greater parts of the cities through
which they flow. The second benefit builds on the first. City admin-
istrators leverage the planning document and the success of the
first project to obtain other public and private funds to continue
their work.

During the era of Syracuse's greatest growth, Onondaga Creek was
the city's "other" waterway, second in every way to the Erie Canal.
This project identifies opportunities to recuperate the creek's
status as both a natural and an infrastructural feature of the urban
landscape with the potential to activate and reorganize the city.
The configuration of the creek today is the cumulative result of
150 years of channelization projects intended to address its
repeated flooding, a phenomenon produced by stormwater runoff
and exacerbated by an overtaxed sewage-treatment system.
To reimagine the creek as part of the city requires addressing its
current character: it receives over one trillion gallons of untreated
wastewater annually from the city's combined sewer overflows,
its feeder brooks are mostly submerged, its flow is dangerously fast,
and the surrounding canopy is overgrown. In its current state, the
creek is unsustainable ecologically, as well as unsafe, unsightly, and
virtually invisible to residents. Yet it has the potential to become
an element of landscape infrastructure that is simultaneously an
educational and a recreational resource.

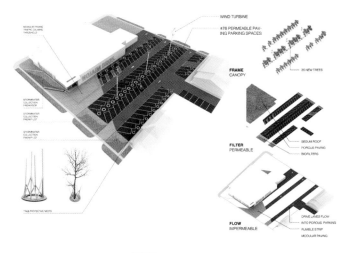

FRAME
CANOPY

FILTER
PERMEABLE

FLOW
IMPERMEABLE

NOJAIMS PARKING LOT PROPOSAL
DIAGRAMS

BENEFITS:
On-site storm water retention and biofiltering, reducing load on sewer system
Generation of on-site, clean wind energy
Improved traffic flows and parking efficiency

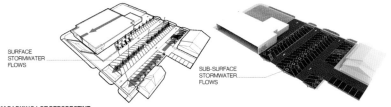

SURFACE
STORMWATER
FLOWS

SUB-SURFACE
STORMWATER
FLOWS

NOJAIM PARKING LOT PERSPECTIVE
WATERSHED AND EXISTING SITE PHOTO

Rendering of part of Onondoga
Creek Walk with proposed
landscape infrastructure

To produce the overall vision for the 6.5 miles of the creek's corridor, the design team mapped the system through the lenses of its ecological, recreational, economic, and educational resources. The resulting design relied on recuperating existing infrastructure and focusing on smaller development projects that can serve as catalysts for future work. These catalytic interventions—projects that accelerate change or recovery—are opportunistic in character and more responsive to changes in local conditions than traditional master planning. For this project we selected four sites distributed along the length of Onondaga Creek to develop conceptual designs. Each site has the distinct potential to sustain a public amenity, increase the visibility of the creek, and support projects for ecological recuperation and economic revitalization.[6]

Modeled on the asset-based approach of social service projects, the design here relies on devising innovative ways to use existing infrastructure beyond its conventional understanding as an underlying functional framework for maintenance and development. Two strategies are foremost in the design. First, landscape infrastructure such as retention ponds, urban forests, recreation facilities, and streetscapes can play a key ecological role. Second, symbiotic infrastructure such as lighting, information systems, and emerging technology can support a new design overlay or function (fig., opposite). The strategy does not attempt to design a continuous, linear greenway; rather, the aim is to propose interventions that are high impact and low cost. Each intervention, which combines an infrastructural and a landscape program, promises not only to recuperate the creek as a primary component of the city but also to spur revitalization of adjacent neighborhoods and commercial areas.

Both the Near Westside Neighborhood Plan and the revitalization efforts for Onondaga Creek hinge on urban landscape as their primary organizing element. More important, these projects show how contemporary practice that expands design ambition to align with available funding streams is one way to improve civic spaces in shrinking cities that would otherwise not have the ability to do so. Syracuse has what in many people's minds are great liabilities—the snow and rain and clouds that challenge its residents' endurance. However, these liabilities can prove to be an asset. By coupling innovative design with available funding, we have the opportunity to produce a reenergized urban realm.

---

1   The UPSTATE: team affiliated with this work includes Julia Czerniak, inaugural director; Joseph Sisko, Jacob Brown, and Trevor Lee; and Brett Seamans and Stephen Klimek (summer). The institute, founded in 2004 by Mark Robbins, former dean of the School of Architecture, initiates, facilitates, and showcases projects that apply innovative design research to economic, environmental, political, and social challenges faced by urban communities. The Metropolitan Development Foundation hired a collaborative team consisting of Julia Czerniak and Mark Linder of CLEAR, Ted Brown of Munly Brown Studio, Joseph Sisko of CELL, and Meredith Perreault and Ed Michelanko of the Onondaga Environmental Institute to pursue a four-stage project that culminated in the report *Onondaga Creek Communities: Projecting Futures for Urban Life* (2009).

2   For more on interdisciplinary speculation about remaking regional shrinking cities, *see Formerly Urban: Projecting Rust Belt Futures*, ed. Julia Czerniak (New York: Princeton Architectural Press, 2012).

3   For more on this program, see http://savetherain.us/.

4   For more examples of "small packages," Julia Czerniak, "Foregrounding" in *Landscape Infrastructure: Case Studies by SWA* (Basel: Birkhäuser, 2010), 20–23.

5   See http://www.dos.ny.gov/communitieswaterfronts/WFRevitalization/LWRP.html for more information on the Local Waterfront Revitalization Program.

6   Since this writing, TeamCLEAR has joined Trowbridge Wolf Michaels Landscape Architects in the next phase of this work.

Campus Projects

1) Life Sciences Landscape
2) Link Hall Addition and Renovation
3) Slocum Hall
4) Carmelo K. Anthony Basketball Center
5) Ernie Davis Hall
6) Huntington Hall
7) Carnegie Library Renovation
8) Campus West Residence Hall
9) Dineen Hall
10) Syracuse University Child Care Campus
11) Bird Library Renovation
12) Indoor Football Practice Facility

City Projects

13) The Warehouse
14) The Bank
15) Link House
16) Syracuse Center of Excellence in Environmental and Energy Systems
17) From the Ground Up Houses: (a) TED House; (b) R-House; (c) Live/Work/Home
18) 601 Tully Community Center
19) Lincoln Supply Building with La Casita Cultural Center
20) Near Westside House Renovations
21) South Side Food Co-op
22) Near Westside Neighborhood Plan
23) WCNY Headquarters

Urban Landscape Projects

24) Syracuse Connective Corridor
25) Syracuse Connective Corridor Competition Winner
26) Onondaga Creek Walk Study

CAMPUS
PROJECTS

LIFE SCIENCES LANDSCAPE

Client
Syracuse University

Architect
Hargreaves Associates

Project start
2006

Project completion
2008 (phase one)

Above: Main pathway from Life
Sciences Building to Slocum Hall

Opposite, top: Diagonal pathways
connecting two corners of campus

Opposite, bottom: New landscape
and benches

The 3.25-acre Life Sciences Landscape transformed parking lots into a college quadrangle, triggered by the completion of the new Life Sciences Complex. Parallel landforms cross the site diagonally, aligned with the regional drumlin field. Their pattern and linearity relate to the program of the building through an allusion to microscopic views of cellular structure. The landforms divert and channel runoff across the site to planting and infiltration trenches to reduce off-site storm loads. Bands of single-species plantings resonate with greenhouse plantings positioned on the roof of the Center for Science and Technology.

LINK HALL ADDITION AND RENOVATION

Client
Syracuse University

Architect
Toshiko Mori Architect

Architect of Record
Einhorn Yaffee Prescott

Project start
2005

Project completion
2008

Cost
$10 million

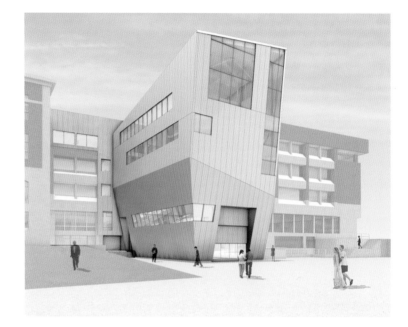

Above: Preliminary rendering

Opposite: Addition under construction, with Slocum Hall at left

Link Hall, built in 1970 by King + King Architects, is home to Syracuse University's L. C. Smith College of Engineering and Computer Science. Adjacent to Slocum Hall, a classical revival building that houses the School of Architecture, the 11,000-square-foot renovation and 9,500-square-foot addition connect the two buildings, enabling interaction and collaboration between faculty and students, engineers and architects.

The faceted form and metal cladding of the new structure contrast with the existing architecture, illuminating the space and creating a focal point for the ensemble. The Structural Engineering High Bay Lab occupies the first floor, with a thirty-foot-high industrial space for materials testing. The third and fourth floors house labs for the Syracuse Center of Excellence in Environmental and Energy Systems, including facilities for indoor environmental and water quality research and a test bed for the study of built environments.

Opposite: View of high bay door

Above: View of new complex

SLOCUM HALL

Client
Syracuse University

Architect
Garrison Architects

Project start
2002

Project completion
2008

Cost
$22 million

Above: *Marcel Breuer and Postwar America* exhibition in Slocum Gallery, 2011

Opposite: Exterior of auditorium from gallery space

Slocum Hall was constructed in 1918 and is listed on the National Register of Historic Places. In the decades that followed its construction, the Beaux-Arts building underwent a series of changes in its mix of tenants and in its form, most notably the loss of its monumental entry stairs and original auditorium, and the closure of its central atrium space. In 1976, Werner Seligmann, then dean of the School of Architecture, began a striking renovation, asserting a modernist clarity within the building and providing spaces that included a reading room, an exhibition gallery, and offices for the school.

The complete renovation by Garrison Architects enhanced and restored original features of the building while updating it technologically, functionally, and aesthetically. The reopening of the central atrium and removal of bearing wall sections allowed pathways for natural light and ventilation, increasing energy efficiency and improving the comfort of occupants. A new auditorium and gallery have been inserted within the historic structure, with greatly expanded studio and research space. Review spaces, a reading room, faculty offices, and a cafe surround the central atrium, providing a setting that encourages interaction among students, faculty, staff, and visitors.

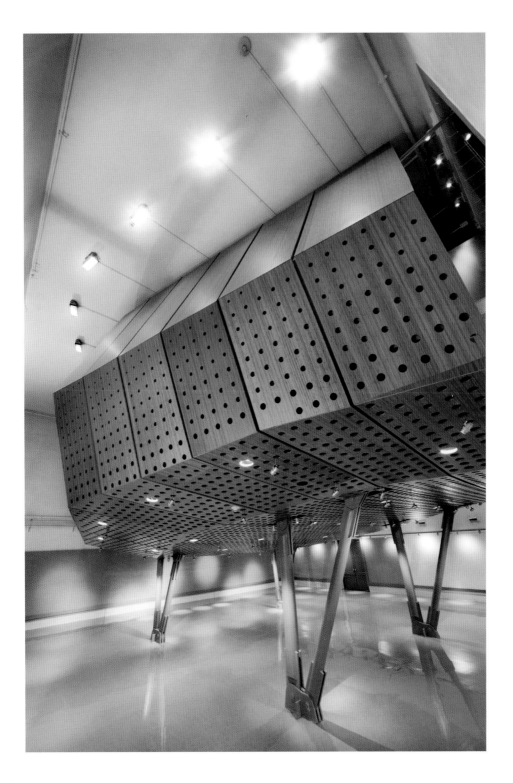

Opposite, top: Atrium
and skylight

Opposite, bottom: Fourth-floor
atrium and stairway

Above: Slocum Auditorium

Left: Slocum Gallery

CARMELO K. ANTHONY BASKETBALL CENTER

Client
Syracuse University

Design Architect
Skidmore, Owings & Merrill

Architect of Record
King + King Architects

Project start
2006

Project completion
2009

Cost
$19 million

Opposite, top: Exterior at night

Opposite, bottom: Rendering of practice area

The 54,000-square-foot Carmelo K. Anthony Basketball Center serves as the training facility for the university's men's and women's basketball programs. The facility features two full practice courts, a strength and conditioning room, an athletic training suite, offices for basketball coaching staff, and locker-room facilities for the teams. Past players are memorialized in the building's entrance, and a spacious, bright entry corridor holds custom-built cases, while framed windows allow viewers glimpses into the practice courts.

The building features a number of sustainable design elements, which have earned it a LEED designation. It uses 30 percent less water and 20 percent less energy than a typical new building, and more than half of the construction and demolition waste was recycled or reused. In addition, some 20 percent of the building's materials are made from recycled products.

The center is the first phase of the new Lampe Athletics Complex master plan, completed by Skidmore, Owings & Merrill, which is meant to improve the university's athletic facilities in order to respond to the demands of competing at the NCAA Division I level and the needs of the general student body. The building is sited in relation to a complex that includes Manley Field House and two auxiliary support facilities, transforming the area into a pedestrian-oriented athletics quad for the university.

ERNIE DAVIS HALL

Client
Syracuse University

Architect
Mack Scogin Merrill Elam Architects

Landscape Architect
Reed Hilderbrand Associates

Engineer
Arup

Project start
2008

Project completion
2009

Cost
$50 million

Above: Night view of main facade

Opposite: Dining hall

The design of Ernie Davis Hall supports wellness by integrating residential life, academic life, and auxiliary social functions. Its placement on campus activates the street edge and creates a court-yard space with DellPlain Hall, a preexisting modernist slab. The 145,000-square-foot facility contains a mix of 60 split-double and 120 single units as well as a 500-seat dining hall, a fitness center, a convenience store, and academic space.

The building programs are linked through a sequence that begins at the southwest entrance. An interior sidewalk rises to become a ramp through the dining hall to the second-level lobby for the residence, which animates the space and provides views of activities inside and outside on campus. Corridor windows, lounges, and studies are strategically placed to maximize daylight, transparency, and views. The building, which earned a LEED Gold certification, incorporates innovative stormwater management, low-water-use fixtures, daylighting, and dining hall efficiencies to reduce food waste and hot-water consumption. An advanced HVAC system also increases energy efficiency. The landscape elements of greens, paths, and terraces reinforce the intention of the building, encouraging social interaction and accommodating an array of informal and structured activities.

Above: Street view of
southwest facade

Right: View from entrance
ramp into dining area

Opposite, top: Dining hall

Opposite, bottom:
View of interior ramp
from street

HUNTINGTON HALL

Client
Syracuse University

Architect
Jonathan Lott

Project start
2012

Projected completion
Entrance/event space: 2013;
auditorium: 2015

Projected cost
Entrance/event space: $1.6 million;
auditorium: $5 million

Opposite, top: Jonathan Lott, winning
entry, rendering of entrance in winter

Opposite, bottom: Jonathan Lott,
winning entry, rendering of entrance
at night

In 2010, three teams were invited to submit designs for a new entry
to the Syracuse University School of Education's Huntington Hall,
located on the edge of campus at the intersection of University
Avenue and Marshall Street, the major social center of "college
town." The boundary between city and campus had been empha-
sized by a fence that surrounded the building and separated it
entirely from the street. The first stage of a multiphase renovation
project, the new entry to the existing nineteenth-century building
would be located at the site of an original stair that was destroyed
during twentieth-century renovations. The interior modifications
needed to accommodate the diverse social functions of the school
and an auditorium are to be added in the near future.

Winning Design: Jonathan Lott
The winning design provides a curved translucent "face" inserted
into a large opening created in the existing facade, which operates
as a historic frame for the new program. The new entrance leads
into a commons, an area for students, faculty, and the public to
gather. When the space is active, it emphasizes the relationship
between the historic image of the building and the current events
of the school. The clear and accessible entry and commons radically change Huntington Hall's relationship to Marshall Street and
the surrounding community.

Competition Entry: Munly Brown Studio with
CELL and VIP Structures
The design proposal offers a complex ramp (with radiant heating)
in lieu of stairs, removing parts of the existing structure and insert-
ing circulatory paths at the main level. Two parallel stripes of light
help activate the space and mark the entrance, visually connecting

the school to University Avenue. With a combination of new landscaping and radical light effects, the design offers the school and university community a new social hub at the north face of the campus.

Competition Entry: French 2D

This proposal negotiates the seven-foot shift between the ground plane and the lobby with a gently terraced stair and ramp system that includes landscape materials and seating areas. The lobby space spills out onto the sidewalk, creating a fluid relationship between interior and exterior. With its faceted, reflective ceiling and light wood floor, the lobby creates a glowing, clean box. Multimedia panels highlight the school's programs and connect its mission to open and public space.

Top: Munly Brown Studio with CELL and VIP Structures, competition entry, rendering of entrance

Above: Munly Brown Studio with CELL and VIP Structures, competition entry, conceptual lighting diagram

Right: Munly Brown Studio with CELL and VIP Structures, competition entry, rendering of interior

Above: French 2D, competition entry, rendering of entrance

Left: French 2D, competition entry, rendering of entrance detail

CARNEGIE LIBRARY RENOVATION

Client
Syracuse University

Architect
Lewis.Tsurumaki.Lewis
(LTL Architects)

Project start
2012

Projected completion
2017

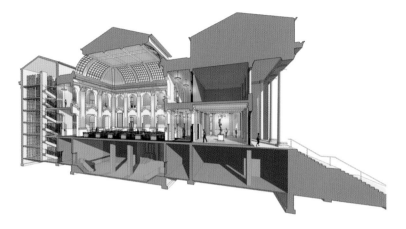

The renovation of the Carnegie Library, built in 1907, includes new classrooms and an auditorium, restores the building's historic public spaces, and reestablishes its original Beaux-Arts plan, with the formal reading room as the central feature of the space. The main entry at the top of the monumental front stone stairs will be reopened, and previous additions that have interrupted the ambulatory around the reading room will be removed. Historic finishes and fixtures will be repaired or replaced, and new energy-efficient materials and technologies sympathetic to the original historic building will be utilized.

Above: Rendering of sectional perspective

Opposite, top: Rendering of second-level hallway

Opposite, bottom: Rendering of glass bays at new entrance

CAMPUS WEST RESIDENCE HALL

Client
Syracuse University

Design Architect
Erdy McHenry Architecture

Architect of Record
Holmes, King, Kallquist & Associates

Project start
2011

Project completion
2012

Cost
$29 million

Above: Rendering of street-level facade

Opposite, clockwise from top: Renderings of main entrance; lobby waiting area; and lobby

The Campus West Residence Hall represents the first example of Syracuse University partnering a nationally recognized architectural firm with a private collegiate-housing development company. This was an effort to provide a high level of design and innovation while satisfying the need to produce affordable campus residences. The building houses full-time and part-time students enrolled in the Syracuse University College of Law, as well as others associated with the college. With 191 fully furnished one-, two-, and four-bedroom apartment units, it provides space for 312 students as well as computer facilities, a fitness room, and study lounges. The ground floor includes 5,000 square feet of retail space and a university store.

The building reinforces the street edge and helps populate the emerging West Campus area, adjacent to the new home of the university's College of Law, Dineen Hall.

DINEEN HALL

Client
Syracuse University
College of Law

Architect
Gluckman Mayner Architects

Landscape Architect
CLEAR

Project start
2012

Projected completion
2014

Projected cost
$67 million

Opposite, top: Rendering of main
facade from street

Opposite, bottom: Rendering of
atrium and auditorium lobby

Dineen Hall is the first academic building constructed on West Campus, a newly planned area of campus that will be a mixed-use, pedestrian-friendly district accessible by public transportation. The building creates a new edge for the campus, with a central atrium space that links a 36,000-square-foot library, courtrooms, a cafe, a 300-seat auditorium, and an event space to accommodate as many as 700 students, 80 faculty, and 95 staff. Classrooms, reading rooms, collaborative learning centers, and study spaces are organized around the perimeter. The building's green roof creates a seasonal outdoor terrace space, while the skylighted atrium introduces natural lighting throughout the building.

Sustainable elements, including a masonry and glass exterior, are designed to achieve LEED Gold certification. A 60-foot-wide landscaped swath adjacent to the building will create a new circulation spine from West Campus to the main campus.

CLEAR's landscape and urban design for Dineen Hall and West Campus includes three distinct areas, with a pedestrian commons, streetscape, and green roof terrace. The commons area is a pathway that is universally accessible and easily maintained. A future east-west retail corridor is planned along Raynor Avenue. The central roof garden on the third floor of Dineen Hall will be planted with a diverse palette of sedges, grasses, and ferns, organized in bold bands.

Above: Rendering of
auditorium from exterior

Right: Rendering of
auditorium lobby

Above: Rendering of view from
interior onto roof garden

Right: Rendering of roof garden

SYRACUSE UNIVERSITY CHILD CARE CAMPUS

Client
Syracuse University

Architect
Munly Brown Studio

Project Status
Unbuilt

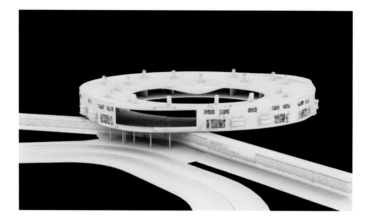

Above: Model rendering
of building

Opposite, top: Rendering of
children's play area

Opposite, bottom:
Rendering of drop-off area

The initial design phase for the new child care campus links two
existing programs located within Syracuse University's South
Campus. The project includes a child care facility, a research arm
of the university's School of Education, and a community center.
Within the natural landscape of drumlins, sports complexes, and
scatter-site housing, the design provides a formal identifying figure
for the child care campus. An ellipse raised above ground houses
classrooms; a gallery for community programs, a kitchen, offices
for counseling services, and a lecture hall are situated at the level
of parking and access.

The two levels are linked internally by a ramp at the hinge of gallery
and ellipse. Each classroom is visually and physically linked to
the internal courtyard and the playing fields. The design embraces
the concept of community and the desire for social interaction at
the scale of campus, courtyard, classrooms, and reading nooks.

BIRD LIBRARY RENOVATION

Client
Syracuse University

Architect
Lewis.Tsurumaki.Lewis
(LTL Architects)

Project start
2012

Projected completion
2014

Above: Rendering of
lower-level classroom

Right: Rendering of study area
and meeting rooms

Opposite, top: Rendering of
study space and hallway

Opposite, bottom: Hybrid floor/
reflected ceiling plan

The renovation of Syracuse University's largest library will include a lecture classroom and a seminar room, each equipped with extensive, state-of-the-art audiovisual equipment. The project capitalizes on the building's existing monumental stairs and walnut paneling by using a system of walnut ceiling and wall fins that radiate outward through the basement level from the stairs. Lounge spaces throughout the basement are created with a variety of seating, from informal groupings to structured reclining seats at the base of the stairs.

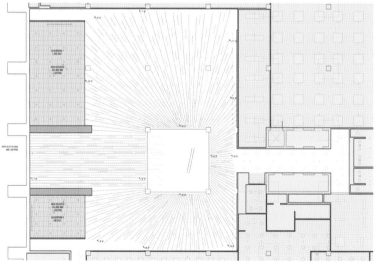

INDOOR FOOTBALL PRACTICE FACILITY

Client
Syracuse University

Project status
Unbuilt

Competitors
Architecture Research Office
Bernheimer Architecture
SHoP Architects

A limited competition was held in 2011 to design a practice facility for the Syracuse University football team, located on the site of the evolving Lampe Athletics Complex, currently an array of various athletic fields and parking lots situated between a residential neighborhood to the west and Manley Field House to the east. The project consists of an indoor practice facility, offices, a weight room, a locker room, and outdoor practice fields. The state-of-the-art, 100,000-square-foot structure will play a key role in the university's ability to compete in football, recruit players, and maintain a national presence in the sport. Three architecture firms—Architecture Research Office, Bernheimer Architecture, and SHoP Architects—submitted designs.

Architecture Research Office (ARO)

Active and passive sustainable strategies are combined with conventional building systems to produce a design that is straightforward and low tech, though its shed roof, entryways, and graphic identity will make the building an iconic piece of architecture within the Lampe Athletics Complex. A high collar of bright orange paneling is inset around the base of the building to lighten its scale. Berms add to the visual character of the project while also calling attention to storage located below ground that collects rainwater to be used on the surrounding lawn fields.

Opposite, top: Architecture Research Office, competition entry, rendering of main entrance

Opposite, bottom: Architecture Research Office, competition entry, rendering of entrance detail

Bernheimer Architecture

The design seeks to create an identity for this new "middle campus" by making an assemblage of disparate buildings into a strong collection. The spaces between the buildings are differentiated with separate vegetation zones and ground surface treatments that reinforce this sense of place and identity and establish the area as a social space for students and student athletics. Column bays and light queen-post trusses occur every ten yards, in alignment with the field landmarks. Translucent wall panels provide a well-lit

neutral background, and daylighting minimizes energy use. The base of the building is formed from precast concrete panels that are patterned with dimples of embedded footballs.

SHoP Architects

The design addresses the immediate needs of a high-performance football facility and incorporates a series of passive sustainable and landscape strategies that will reduce the building's overall carbon footprint. Louvers integrated into the building-scale signage along the east and west elevations of the facility provide natural ventilation to reduce cooling loads during the summer months. Natural daylight is provided through a series of translucent skylights in the roof and transparent openings at grade. The primary structural system for the building consists of steel trusses that span the practice field, with each frame taking the form of a single gable roof.

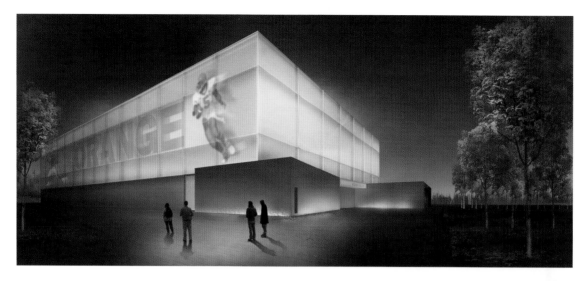

Above: Bernheimer Architecture,
competition entry, rendering of main
entrance showing projection at night

Right: Bernheimer Architecture,
competition entry, rendering of
rear entrance

Opposite, top: SHoP Architects,
competition entry, aerial rendering
of complex

Opposite, bottom: SHoP Architects,
competition entry, rendering of
complex at twilight

CITY PROJECTS

THE WAREHOUSE

Client
Syracuse University

Design Architect
Gluckman Mayner Architects

Architect of Record
VIP Structures

Project start
2005

Project completion
2007

Cost
$9 million

Above: Warehouse building
before renovation

Opposite: View of Warehouse, Fayette
Street, and Onondaga Street Walk

The renovation of an underutilized 140,000-square-foot warehouse building in downtown Syracuse provided a temporary home for the entire Syracuse University School of Architecture during the renovation of its on-campus home. In addition, it housed community art spaces and library storage and provided space for the university's College of Visual and Performing Arts. The existing clay-tile facade was replaced on two sides with an aluminum-frame shop front, with variously tinted double-glazed windows, punctuated by bright orange translucent panels. The windows afford views out over the city, and at night, the studio's active interior spaces are visible from the street.

The fast-tracked project, built in ten months, created the first major presence for the university in downtown Syracuse in recent history. Located in Armory Square, one of the city's few pedestrian-friendly neighborhoods, the building has created a hub of activity at the edge of the historic center. It has also stimulated a number of private real estate development projects. Today, the Warehouse is home to the School of Architecture's UPSTATE: A Center for Design, Research, and Real Estate as well as its visiting-critic studios; the Goldring Arts Journalism Program; the departments of art, design, and transmedia of the College of Visual and Performing Arts; and the offices of the Near Westside Initiative and the Warehouse Gallery.

The Warehouse also serves as a major node on the Connective Corridor, which links the university and downtown Syracuse, with a new park space designed by Olin Partnership.

Top: East facade with
glare-resistant blue glass and
amber Panelite windows

Above: View looking east
from top floor

Right: Interior of reading
room at night

Opposite, top: *Making
Frames* exhibition by
Gluckman Mayner Architecture
in Warehouse Gallery

Opposite, bottom:
Warehouse cafe

THE BANK

Client
Robbins Hanover Square LLC

Architect
Mark Robbins with
Fiedler Marciano Architecture

Project start
2005

Project completion
2007

Above left: Dinner party in vaulted living space

Above right: Beaux-Arts facade from Hanover Square

Opposite: Living and dining areas facing out over Hanover Square

Built in 1898 as the Bank of Syracuse, the building is an innovative steel-and-concrete structure designed in an exuberant Beaux-Arts style by Albert Brockway, an associate of the architect Ernest Flagg. The Bank is situated on Hanover Square, one of the oldest and most intact mixed-use areas in Syracuse, whose downtown core has only recently begun to accommodate increasing numbers of residents.

In successive alterations, the interior of the building had been divided into three separate levels and eventually subdivided into a series of small, dark, carpeted offices with hung ceilings, covering most of its ornamental plaster and marble. After the nearly vacant building was acquired in 2005, selective demolition exposed the 75-foot-long barrel-vaulted ceiling of the former banking hall and fragments of marble mosaic and ornament. The first floor was cleared to create an open loft space for offices, and the upper level was converted to a residence. New quartersawn oak flooring was installed over the length of the space, which is heated with a radiant system. A white abstract block accommodates baths and a kitchen and laundry, separating the large gallery hall from the living space and library.

LINK HOUSE

Client
Home HeadQuarters

Design Team
Lubrano Ciavarra Architects; Syracuse University School of Architecture students; Home HeadQuarters; VIP Structures; and Haven Homes

Project start
2008

Project completion
2009

Cost
$175,000

Above: Rendering of main living area

Opposite, clockwise from top: Exterior of house in context; crane lifting roof into place; students in front of house during construction

An options studio at the Syracuse University School of Architecture offered students the opportunity to participate in the design and construction of a 1,400-square-foot, single-family home on the city's Near Westside. Led by the architects and visiting critics Anne Marie Lubrano and Lea Ciavarra, the studio was based on a seminar about innovative and energy-efficient approaches to the renovation of typical wood-frame housing stock. The class chose to explore the potential of prefabrication and worked closely with a regional manufacturer, Haven Homes, to realize the project.

Built on an infill site in this older neighborhood, the project marked the school's first collaboration with Home HeadQuarters, a private nonprofit housing provider, and VIP Structures, a contractor. Students and faculty were involved in each phase of the work, from client contact to materials research and fabrication.

SYRACUSE CENTER OF EXCELLENCE IN ENVIRONMENTAL AND ENERGY SYSTEMS

Client
Syracuse University

Design Architect
Toshiko Mori Architect

Architect of Record
Ashley McGraw Architect

Design Team
7 Group (LEED Consultant);
Arup & Partners (Mechanical,
Electrical, Plumbing, and
Structural Engineering)

Project start
2005

Project completion
2010

Cost
$41 million

The Syracuse Center of Excellence in Environmental and Energy Systems headquarters is a research center for a federation of more than 200 institutes, corporations, and academic programs that collaborate on the research and promotion of environmentally responsible technologies. Considered a living lab, the 55,000-square-foot facility is located on a remediated brownfield that anchors the corridor connecting the city center and the university campus. Many of the lab environments are on public display, visually communicating the research being conducted within the institution. Laboratories are organized along a circulation path that acts as a gallery, creating an open and inviting architecture to draw the public to the site. Among the building's labs is the Carrier Total Indoor Environmental Quality Laboratory, dedicated to conducting controlled experiments on the human response to indoor environments, which is the only research facility of its kind in the world.

This LEED Platinum–certified building counts extensive sustainable design elements. Its narrow width takes advantage of daylight, natural ventilation, and panoramic views. Long facades on the north and south benefit from the movement of the sun, optimizing solar radiation year-round, and the building is insulated by a green roof, which is solar and wind-power ready.

Above: Main facade and entry
from street

Left: Aerial view of building
in context

Page 100, top: Ramped
green roof

Page 100, bottom:
Flexible gathering space

Page 101: Ramped roof in winter

LINCOLN SUPPLY BUILDING

Client
Near Westside Initiative

Architect
Brininstool + Lynch

Project start
2009

Project completion
2010

Cost
$4 million

Above: Street view

Opposite: Building exterior
with green screen

The renovation of the former Lincoln Supply Warehouse, entailing a complete restructuring of the building, was the first large-scale, mixed-use project by the Near Westside Initiative. Ranging from 1,100 to 1,300 square feet, ten live/work lofts occupy the upper floors, generating revenue that supports the management and upkeep of the building. The first two floors house two nonprofit organizations, Say Yes to Education and La Casita Cultural Center.

The 30,000-square-foot building features energy-efficient geothermal heating and cooling, high-efficiency fixtures and appliances, a planted green screen that helps cool the building, and stormwater retention to eliminate site water from city and county sewer systems. This renovation of an underutilized industrial building helps anchor the site with residential tenants and institutional tenants dedicated to the arts and education.

LA CASITA CULTURAL CENTER

Client
Syracuse University

Architect
Jonathan Lott

Project start
2009

Project completion
2012

Cost
$150,000

Above: Main hallway with bookshelves

Opposite, top: Main hallway

Opposite, bottom: Auditorium and presentation space

Located in the Near Westside neighborhood of Syracuse, the center serves the Latino community as an intergenerational meeting place by providing cultural and educational programs. The 5,000-square-foot space is located on the first floor of the Lincoln Supply Building, which includes loft apartments and offices on the upper floors. Partitions and curtains in bright hues close off areas defined for an art gallery, bilingual library, informal classroom, kitchen, and performance space. The center offers a dual-language reading program and a literacy and writing program for students preparing to enter high school, and encourages exchange and collaboration between the university and the neighborhood community.

Opposite: Community library
and exhibition space

Left: Hallway and community
gathering area

Below: Presentation and
gathering space

FROM THE GROUND UP HOUSES

The From the Ground Up houses are the result of an international design competition held in Syracuse in 2008—initiated by the Syracuse University School of Architecture, with Home HeadQuarters, a private nonprofit housing provider, and the Syracuse Center of Excellence in Environmental and Energy Systems—with the goal of creating new models for affordable high-performance green homes in urban residential neighborhoods. Developed and built on vacant infill sites in the Near Westside neighborhood of Syracuse, these single-family houses were designed to be energy and cost efficient, as well as sensitive to the scale and fabric of the community. The projects demonstrate that good design and advanced technology are essential in the creation of sustainable prototypes. They provide an ambitious but feasible vision for the redevelopment of urban neighborhoods throughout the United States.

From the Ground Up houses:

Live/Work/Home by Cook + Fox Architects with Terrapin Bright Green

R-House by Architecture Research Office and Della Valle Bernheimer

TED House by Onion Flats

Opposite, clockwise from top: Live/Work/Home; TED House; R-House

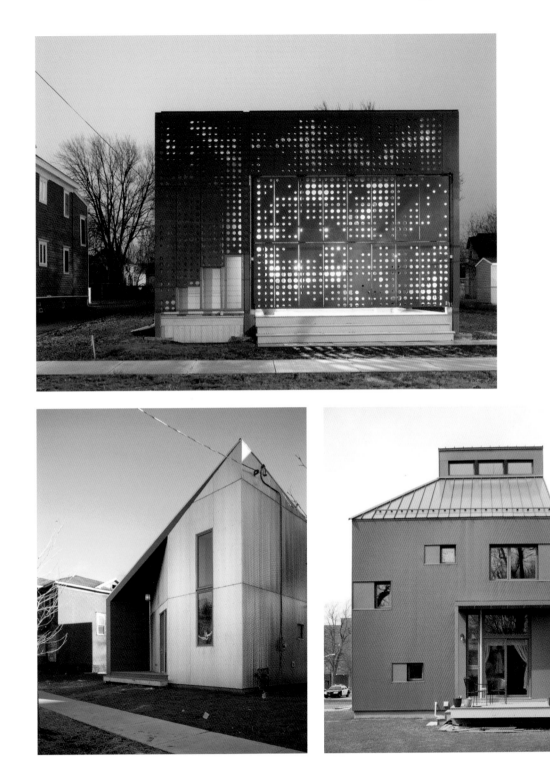

LIVE/WORK/HOME

Client
Home HeadQuarters

Architect
Cook + Fox Architects
with Terrapin Bright Green

Project start
2009

Project completion
2010

Cost
$150,000

This single-story, flat-roof design is highly flexible and can be transformed to accommodate the changing needs of the residents, whether a family with children, an extended family unit, or students, and can easily be converted to function as a home-based small business or artist's studio. The house is made of structural insulated panels and is heated passively. Adjustable reflective screening and skylights fill the space with dappled lighting.

Above: View of street from porch

Opposite, clockwise from top: Porch closed at night; detail of perforated sunshading panels; rear facade

R-HOUSE

Client
Home HeadQuarters

Architects
Architecture Research Office
and Della Valle Bernheimer

Project start
2009

Project completion
2010

Cost
$150,000

Right: View of entrance from street

Opposite, clockwise from top: Rear
facade and neighboring TED House;
view of rear windows looking toward
street; living room

This two-story house transforms a typical gabled roof into a simple
folded surface that recalls the appearance and scale of neighboring houses. Its flexible layout accommodates two, three, or four
bedrooms within the same shell. The passive solar strategy utilizes
a well-insulated envelope, airtight construction, an efficient small
heating system, controlled ventilation, and windows that optimize
solar gain, requiring a negligible amount of heating energy.

TED HOUSE

Client
Home HeadQuarters

Architect
Onion Flats

Project start
2009

Project completion
2010

Cost
$150,000

Above: Rear facade and
neighboring R-House

Opposite, clockwise from top:
Rear and side facades;
upstairs landing; view of
upstairs reading loft

TED House was designed to be built in three different ways: stick framing, modular construction, or structural insulated panels. The structure combines a thick shell and active solar heating to create an energy-efficient house. The heating system uses water heated through solar-tubing panels mounted on the roof and radiant tubing in all the floors. The three-story, gabled-roof structure creates an atrium to pull heat out of the living area during the summer months, making a space that is energy efficient year-round. The versatile design can easily be transformed into a two- to four-bedroom, a duplex, or a home office/studio with residence above.

601 TULLY COMMUNITY CENTER

Client
Near Westside Initiative

Architects
Marion Wilson and students from the School of Architecture's Social Sculpture Class with Anda French

Project start
2009

Project completion
2011

Cost
$300,000

Above: Community event in first-floor meeting area

Opposite: Attic office and exhibition space

601 Tully is a community center for the arts within a renovated wood-frame house in Syracuse's Near Westside neighborhood. The renovation of the building itself is the result of a two-year collaboration between Marion Wilson, associate professor at the Syracuse University School of Education, and Anda French, assistant professor at the university's School of Architecture, as part of Wilson's social sculpture course. An interdisciplinary team of Syracuse University students designed and built parts of the center and many of its furnishings, and they were involved in every stage of the process, from enlisting community support and attending zoning committee meetings to laying floorboards. The center features an art gallery, classrooms, gardens, and a cafe.

NEAR WESTSIDE HOUSE RENOVATIONS

Client
Home HeadQuarters

Design Team
Stelle Architects; Timothy Stenson; Syracuse University School of Architecture students; Home HeadQuarters; and VIP Structures

Project start
2010

Project completion
2012

Cost
607–609 Otisco Street: $107,000;
615 Otisco Street: $175,000

Above: Rendering of 615 Otisco Street

Opposite: Rendering of 607–609 Otisco Street

Frederick Stelle, principal of Stelle Architects, and Timothy Stenson, Syracuse University School of Architecture undergraduate chair, were paired for visiting-critic studios that developed designs for the renovation of two residential properties in the Near Westside neighborhood of Syracuse—a single-family house and a two-family house. The studio divided into small "offices" of working teams, each assigned one project, and each advancing through schematic design and design development with particular attention to budget, realities of the local housing market, and its construction capacity. Students also participated in administering the construction of the projects.

The intention was to preserve the structures' historic shells and insert new spatial and material elements without altering the neighborhood's existing context and urban fabric. This studio was part of an ongoing effort by the School of Architecture to bring real-life experience to the curriculum and more broadly by Syracuse University to partner in the revitalization of the Near Westside neighborhood.

SOUTHSIDE FOOD CO-OP

Client
Southside Community Coalition

Architect
sekou cooke STUDIO

Project start
2012

Projected completion
2013

Projected cost
$1.2 million

Above: Rendering
of main facade

Opposite: Rendering
of co-op interior

The Southside Food Co-op is an owner-operated, community-based grocery for the residents of this historic Syracuse neighborhood. The first new construction in the neighborhood in more than thirty years, it will provide fresh fruit and produce in an area currently considered a food desert.

The main volume of the building is wrapped in corrugated aluminum, which is folded asymmetrically to promote passive heat reduction and to maximize the roof area designated for photovoltaic panels. The roof is also designed to reclaim and recycle stormwater runoff. The two adjoining volumes are clad in a fiber cement rain screen and house service programs and a cafe facing South Salina Street. The interior display walls, built-in seating, and cash register storage units are part of a design/build package by the architect. The exterior site work will include porously paved parking spaces, an outdoor event space with fixed seating, bicycle parking, and new street trees.

NEAR WESTSIDE NEIGHBORHOOD PLAN

Client
Near Westside Initiative

Design
UPSTATE: A Center for Design,
Research, and Real Estate

Project start
2009

Projected completion
Ongoing

Opposite, top to bottom:
Renderings of crosswalk;
sidewalk improvement;
and rain garden and park

Conceived as an alternative to the conventional master plan, the Near Westside Neighborhood Plan proposes contemporary solutions grounded in the local assets of a postindustrial neighborhood.

Syracuse, like every sixth city in the world, can be defined as a "shrinking city," characterized by the loss of urban fabric, social welfare networks, and basic services, as well as the erosion of public school systems. The loss of the traditional economic base combined with increasing amounts of tax-delinquent and vacant land and failing infrastructure has a direct impact on public health, public safety, and the environment. This project stresses the importance of design and innovation in reconceiving and rebuilding shrinking cities in general and the Near Westside neighborhood of Syracuse specifically. It recognizes that although a shrinking city is not a dying one, the potential for active urban life requires developing new design strategies that foreground the cultural, human, and infrastructural assets of a place.

The Near Westside Neighborhood Plan grew out of a 2009 landscape-focused architecture studio that asked students to explore ways to develop urbanity in the postindustrial city. Their analysis, coupled with input from a small group of professionals, local experts, city advisers, and neighborhood residents, helped identify key planning issues and target outcomes. The proposed framework of big and small moves is organized around five categories: green infrastructure, circulation networks, lighting and security, zoning and land use, and signage and wayfinding. The plan's primary objective is to create an alternative approach to neighborhood planning that is landscape based, economically and environmentally regenerative, and scalable.

WCNY HEADQUARTERS

Client
Near Westside Initiative

Design Architect
Koning Eizenberg Architecture

Architect of Record
King + King Architects

Project start
2011

Projected completion
2013

Projected cost
$20 million

Above: Buildings before renovation

Opposite: Aerial rendering
of project site and elevated railroad

This project relocates the headquarters of Central New York's public television station, WCNY, from a northern suburb of Syracuse to a site on Syracuse's Near Westside. It involves the reuse and selective demolition of a cluster of warehouse buildings, which will now house TV and radio studios, a cafe, an auditorium, and office and educational spaces, as well as new construction for studios and control rooms. The renovation also includes the creation of headquarters for an international adult literacy organization, Pro-Literacy, and residential lofts.

WCNY is designed to be a public place, with a relationship to the community at street level that is activated by a cafe, radio studios, and views into the media operations. Educational programs occupy the remaining ground-floor area. The new building and its location help position WCNY as a leading cultural anchor as well as a vibrant presence in the Near Westside neighborhood and the region.

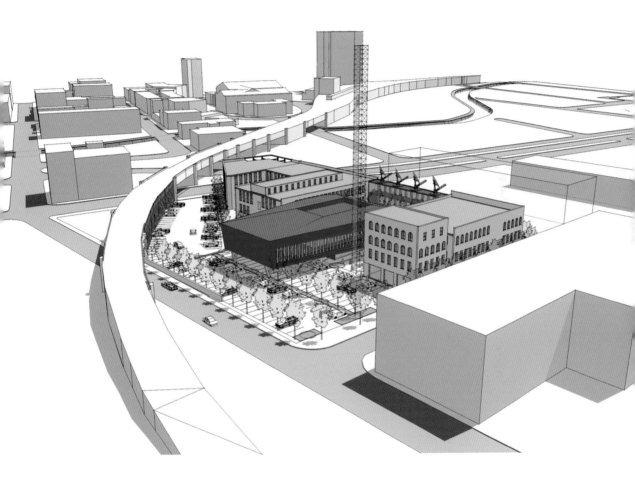

This page, top to bottom: Renderings of WCNY Headquarters plaza; courtyard; lighting plan; and front entrance and landscape

Opposite, top: North facade of renovated Case Supply building during construction

Opposite, bottom: South facade of renovated Case Supply building during construction

URBAN
LANDSCAPE
PROJECTS

SYRACUSE CONNECTIVE CORRIDOR

Client
Syracuse University

Design Team
Barton & Loguidice; Olin Partnership; and UPSTATE: A Center for Design, Research, and Real Estate

Consultants
Pentagram; Tillett Lighting Design

Project start
2008

Completion of phase one
2012

In March 2005 Syracuse University, National Grid, and the former congressman James Walsh proposed the Syracuse Connective Corridor to create closer connections between University Hill and downtown Syracuse. In the summer of 2006 a competition sponsored by National Grid was held to design a landscape and transit system linking the people and activities of University Hill and downtown, featuring existing arts institutions, entertainment venues, and public spaces. The intention of the competition was to bring together Syracuse's public, private, community, and business sectors to strengthen the community, connect residents with cultural venues, and promote further economic development. Competition finalists included Deborah Berke and Partners Architects with Olin Partnership; Rockwell Group with SYSTEMarchitects, DIRT Studio, and Light Projects Ltd.; and Sasaki Associates. The winning entry was a design by Field Operations and CLEAR called the Syracuse L.

2006 Competition Winner
The winning competition design from Field Operations and CLEAR (see pages 136–37) included a multimodal transportation circuit of bus, car, bike, and pedestrian lanes that creates a legible, resilient, and brandable loop connecting Syracuse's arts and cultural institutions. The Syracuse L was proposed as both a place and a path of exchange—of people, ideas, goods, and services—that welcomes diverse populations from all parts of the city and county. Events activate the transit loop: from interactive fountains, movie screenings, and tailgating on a lushly planted "parking carpet" to technology pavilions that link Syracuse residents to the world through Internet ports. It offered another layer in the history of transportation infrastructure that shaped the city following the Erie Canal, the railroad, and the road system.

Because of budget constraints, it was not possible to move ahead with the Syracuse L.

Ongoing Project

During the next phase, a request for proposals went out and a new design team was selected for the project. The new design aims to create a safe and enjoyable urban environment, enhancing Syracuse's distinct character and history while also improving ease of movement throughout the heart of the city.

Partners in the project include Syracuse University, former congressman James Walsh, Senator Charles Schumer, former senator Hillary Rodham Clinton, the city of Syracuse, National Grid (the lead corporate partner), and Time Warner Cable. During the academic year, Centro and Syracuse University offer the Connective Corridor shuttle bus, a free service to all riders commuting between destinations along the corridor.

The first phase consists of three principal streetscapes and parks, as well as lighting, public art, and info spots, a series of interactive kiosks. These new landscapes further connect and highlight the city's economic, cultural, and evolving residential assets.

The Connective Corridor has three main components:

The Connector: The primary infrastructural route consisting of a dedicated bike lane, lighting, green infrastructure, and a new plan for trees along the street to reinforce the interconnectedness of the cultural institutions that are located between the university and the downtown area.

The Civic Strip: A 1.5-mile band of pedestrian-oriented streetscape improvements that intersects the Connector to establish a visible link with the civic institutions.

Activity Nodes: A series of public spaces along the Connector and the Civic Strip that are designed to enhance public interaction within the city, focused on technology, the environment, or a specific institutional program.

ONGOING PROJECT

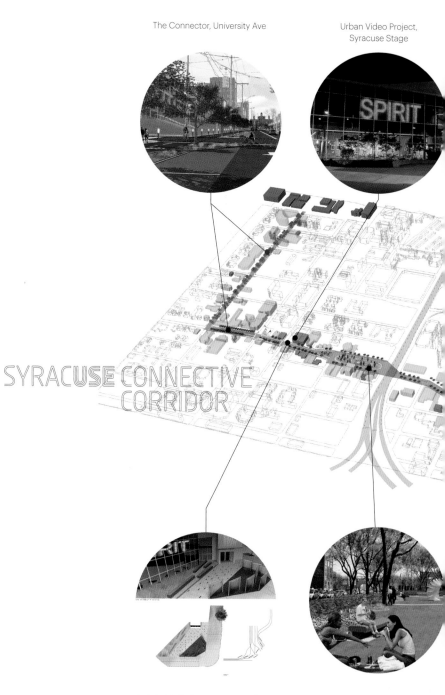

The Connector, University Ave

Urban Video Project,
Syracuse Stage

Barton & Loguidice, Olin Partnership,
and UPSTATE:, schematic drawing
showing activity nodes for the
Connective Corridor as it unfolds

Activity Node, Syracuse Stage Plaza

Activity Node, Forman Park

Urban Video Project,
Everson Plaza

Civic Strip, Jefferson Connection

Activity Node, WCNY Courtyard

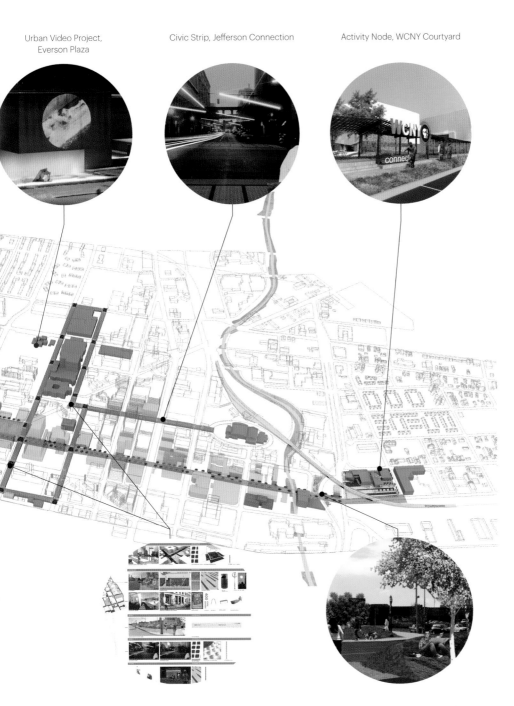

Civic Strip, Typology Diagram

Activity Node, Warehouse Cafe

ONGOING PROJECT

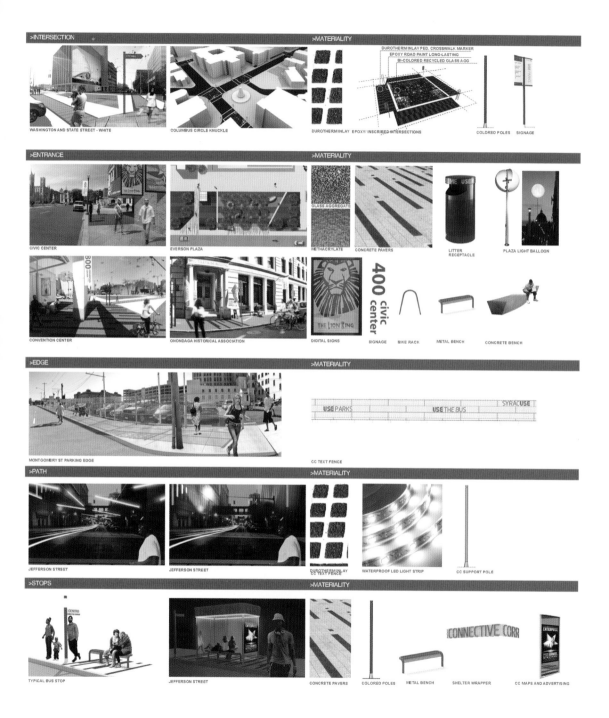

>INTERSECTION   >MATERIALITY

WASHINGTON AND STATE STREET - WHITE

COLUMBUS CIRCLE KNUCKLE

DUROTHERM INLAY PED. CROSSWALK MARKER
EPOXY ROAD PAINT LONG-LASTING
BI-COLORED RECYCLED GLASS AGG.

DUROTHERM INLAY EPOXY INSCRIBED INTERSECTIONS

COLORED POLES   SIGNAGE

>ENTRANCE   >MATERIALITY

CIVIC CENTER

EVERSON PLAZA

GLASS AGGREGATE

METHACRYLATE

CONCRETE PAVERS

LITTER RECEPTACLE

PLAZA LIGHT BALLOON

CONVENTION CENTER

ONONDAGA HISTORICAL ASSOCIATION

DIGITAL SIGNS

400 civic center

THE LION KING

SIGNAGE   BIKE RACK   METAL BENCH   CONCRETE BENCH

>EDGE   >MATERIALITY

MONTGOMERY ST PARKING EDGE

USE PARKS   USE THE BUS   SYRACUSE

CC TEXT FENCE

>PATH   >MATERIALITY

JEFFERSON STREET

JEFFERSON STREET

DUROTHERM INLAY
CC TEXT FENCE

WATERPROOF LED LIGHT STRIP

CC SUPPORT POLE

>STOPS   >MATERIALITY

TYPICAL BUS STOP

JEFFERSON STREET

CONCRETE PAVERS

COLORED POLES   METAL BENCH   SHELTER WRAPPER   CC MAPS AND ADVERTISING

CONNECTIVE CORR

Above: Urban Video Project at the Everson Museum on the Connective Corridor

Left: Plaza entrance to Syracuse Stage on the Connective Corridor

Opposite: Barton & Loguidice, Olin Partnership, and UPSTATE:, Syracuse Civic Strip concepts

COMPETITION WINNER

Above: Field Operations with CLEAR, competition entry, rendering of Syracuse L, East Genesee Street, and bike path looking west

Right: Field Operations with CLEAR, competition entry, axonometric plan of Syracuse L

Opposite, top: Field Operations with CLEAR, competition entry, rendering of Syracuse L winter activities

Opposite, bottom: Field Operations with CLEAR, competition entry, rendering of East Genesee Street, with light gallery

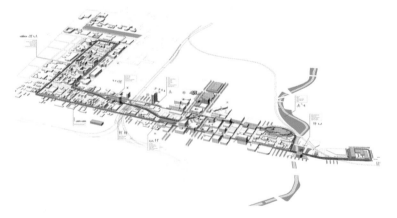

ONONDAGA CREEK WALK STUDY

Client
Metropolitan Development
Foundation

Design Team
Julia Czerniak and Mark Linder
of CLEAR; Ted Brown of Munly
Brown Studio; and Joe Sisko
of CELL, with the Onondaga
Environmental Institute

Project start
2008

Project completion
2009

Opposite, clockwise from top left:
Renderings of Onondaga Creek
Walk Study sites A, B, C, and D

Syracuse University School of Architecture faculty members Julia Czerniak and Mark Linder of CLEAR, Ted Brown of Munly Brown Studio, and Joe Sisko of CELL, with the Onondaga Environmental Institute, completed a yearlong study of Onondaga Creek, the main waterway running through the city of Syracuse. The study was part of the Metropolitan Development Foundation's Creative Communities project, funded by the Ford Foundation to "produce conceptual designs for four sites along the Onondaga Creek corridor based on a comprehensive evaluation of ongoing initiatives and the creek's latent potential, as landscape infrastructure, to support sustainable urban revitalization."

Building on the growing interest in the creek and employing catalytic landscape infrastructure strategies, this project located discrete, easily acquired sites along the length of the creek to maximize results for a relatively small investment. Rather than envisioning the recuperation of the creek as a large-scale design for a continuous infrastructure or greenway that extends the length of Onondaga Lake, this project identified sites of intensity where numerous factors coalesced: the opportunity for environmental restoration and recreational activities, proximity to educational institutions, and the potential for economic development.

Each intervention utilized the creek as a primary infrastructural and visual component of the city to spur revitalization of adjacent neighborhoods and commercial areas. The team selected four promising sites, then proposed a conceptual design for each that demonstrates the potential for the recuperation of infrastructure to spur development both directly (by consolidating underutilized public, vacant, or tax-delinquent lands) and indirectly (by increasing the visibility, accessibility, and legibility of the creek). Each of the four designs includes a combined infrastructural and landscape program to be constructed in three phases.

NOTES ON
CONTRIBUTORS

Barry Bergdoll is the Philip Johnson Chief Curator of Architecture and Design at the Museum of Modern Art and professor of modern architectural history at Columbia University. He has organized, curated, and consulted on many major exhibitions of architecture at MoMA, including *Henri Labrouste: Structure Brought to Light*; *Le Corbusier: An Atlas of Modern Landscapes*; *194X–9/11: American Architects and the City*; *Bauhaus 1919–1933: Workshops for Modernity*; *Home Delivery: Fabricating the Modern Dwelling*; *Lost Vanguard: Soviet Modernist Architecture, 1922–32*; and *Mies in Berlin*, with Terence Riley. Among the award-winning books Bergdoll has written or contributed to are *Bauhaus 1919–1933: Workshops for Modernity*; *Home Delivery: Fabricating the Modern Dwelling*; and *Mies in Berlin*. He has served as chairman of the department of art history and archaeology at Columbia University (2004–7) and president of the Society of Architectural Historians (2006–8), in addition to participating in juries, editorial boards, and professional organizations.

Nancy Cantor is chancellor and president of Syracuse University. She also lectures and writes extensively on the role of universities as anchor institutions in their communities, as well as other crucial issues in higher education. Cantor is cochair of the American Commonwealth Partnership's Presidents Council, a member of the steering committee of the Anchor Institutions Task Force, and cochair of the Central New York Regional Economic Development Council, a post to which she was appointed by New York governor Andrew Cuomo. Prior to her tenure at Syracuse, she served as chancellor of the University of Illinois at Urbana-Champaign and provost and executive vice president for academic affairs at the University of Michigan. Cantor holds a PhD in psychology and is a fellow of the American Academy of Arts and Sciences and a member of the Institute of Medicine of the National Academy of Sciences. In 2008, she received the Carnegie Corporation's Academic Leadership Award.

Julia Czerniak is professor of architecture at Syracuse University and was the inaugural director of UPSTATE: A Center for Design, Research, and Real Estate. She is also a registered landscape architect and founder of CLEAR, an interdisciplinary design practice. Czerniak is the editor of three books—*Large Parks, Case: Downsview Park Toronto*, and *Formerly Urban: Projecting Rust Belt Futures*—which focus on the relationship between landscape and cities. She has also contributed essays to *Landscape Alchemy: The Work of Hargreaves Associates, Fertilizers: Olin Eisenman, The Landscape Urbanism Reader*, and *Assemblage 34*. With Marpillero Pollak Architects, she won the artNET Public Art Landscape Design Competition in Toledo, Ohio, and was a winner of the Architectural League of New York's Young Architects Forum competition in 2001. Czerniak has exhibited at the Architectural League, the Storefront for Art and Architecture, the Graham Foundation for Advanced Studies, the Van Alen Institute, Castle Gallery, Galleria Frau, and Gallery Joe.

Mark Robbins is executive director of the International Center of Photography in New York and former dean of the Syracuse University School of Architecture and the university's senior adviser for architecture and urban initiatives. Previously, he was director of design at the National Endowment for the Arts, curator of architecture at the Wexner Center for the Arts in Columbus, Ohio, and an associate professor in the Knowlton School of Architecture at The Ohio State University. Robbins has been a visiting critic at the University of Virginia, the Georgia Institute of Technology, and the Graduate School of Design at Harvard University. Notable among his awards are the Rome Prize from the American Academy in Rome and grants from the NEA, the Graham Foundation, and the state arts councils of Ohio and New York. Robbins was a fellow in the visual arts at the Radcliffe Institute for Advanced Study at Harvard University in 2002–3. His book *Households* was published by the Monacelli Press in 2006.

Illustration Credits

32, 58, 60, 61, 90, 92 bottom, 93 bottom, 94, 97 bottom, 104–6, 116, 117, 124, 135: Syracuse University, photographs by Steve Sartori

36: Fiedler Marciano Architecture

37, 63 top, 99, 100, 102, 103, 107: Magda Biernat

44, 45, 48–49, 123, 126, 127, 132–34: UPSTATE:

46, 139: CLEAR, Munly Brown Studio, CELL

52, 53: Hargreaves Associates

54: Toshiko Mori Architect

55, 101: Iwan Baan

56, 57: John Griebsch

59: David Joseph

63 bottom: SOM

64, 66 top: Jamie Young

65, 66 bottom, 67 top: Mack Scogin Merrill Elam Architects

67 bottom: Maren Guse

69: Jonathan Lott

70, 80, 81: Munly Brown Studio

71: French 2D Design

72, 73, 82, 83: Lewis.Tsurumaki.Lewis

74, 75: Erdy McHenry Architecture

77, 78 bottom: Gluckman Mayner Architects

78 top, 79: CLEAR

85: Architecture Research Office

86: Bernheimer Architecture

87: SHoP Architects

91, 92 top, 93 top: David Heald

95: Stewart Cairns

96: Lubrano Ciavarra Architects

97 top: Mark Robbins

109–15: Richard Barnes

118, 119: Syracuse University School of Architecture

120, 121: sekou cooke STUDIO

125: Koning Eizenberg Architecture

136, 137: Field Operations with CLEAR